Managing Editor
Mara Ellen Guckian

Editors in Chief
Karen J. Goldfluss, M.S. Ed.
Ina Massler Levin, M.A.

Cover Artist
Diem Pascarella

Creative Director
Karen J. Goldfluss, M.S. Ed.

Art Coordinator
Renée Mc Elwee

Illustrator
Kelly McMahon

Imaging
James Edward Grace
Craig Gunnell
Rosa C. See

Publisher
Mary D. Smith, M.S. Ed.

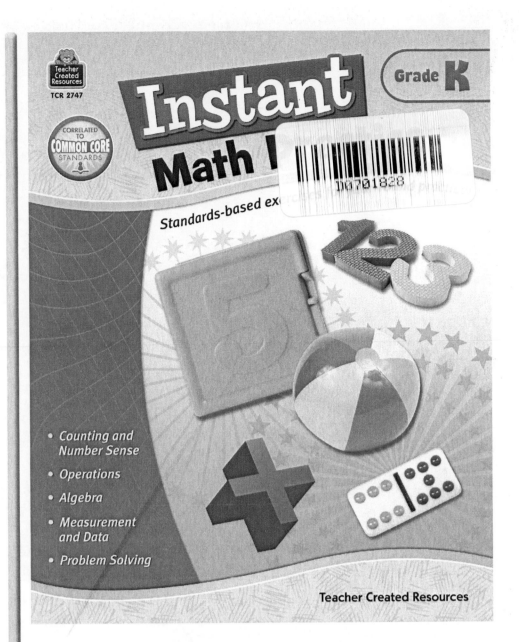

TCR 2747

CORRELATED TO COMMON CORE STANDARDS

Instant
Math

Grade **K**

Standards-based ex...

- Counting and Number Sense
- Operations
- Algebra
- Measurement and Data
- Problem Solving

Teacher Created Resources

Written and Compiled by
Mara Ellen Guckian

Teacher Created Resources
12621 Western Avenue
Garden Grove, CA 92841
www.teachercreated.com

ISBN: 978-1-4206-2747-3

©2013 Teacher Created Resources
Reprinted, 2019
Made in U.S.A.

Teacher Created Resources

Table of Contents

Introduction

The *Instant Math Practice* series was developed to support classroom math curriculums and to provide students with opportunities to master and retain important math skills. Each page was designed to encourage students to discover mathematical relationships and to recognize the value of math in everyday life.

The standards-based pages can be used in whole-class situations to reinforce new concepts being taught. They can also be used in centers to provide additional practice or for more specific one-on-one Response to Intervention (RTI) support.

This series challenges students to *think* about math, not just memorize facts. The units are scaffolded to build upon prior knowledge. Each practice page focuses on specific math skills. *Instant Math Practice (K)* includes the following topics: Number Sense 0–30, Addition, Subtraction, and Word Problems.

Number and word problems are presented in a variety of ways and incorporate important math vocabulary. The more math vocabulary is incorporated into daily language, the more students will internalize the math they are learning. A broad knowledge of math vocabulary benefits students during testing, as well.

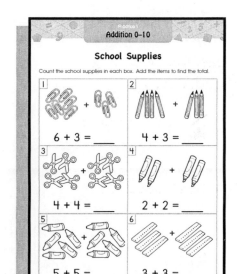

As active learners completing each page, students will develop a strong understanding of grade-level math concepts. And as students progress, their problem-solving skills will improve in math and across other curricular areas, thus boosting their overall confidence and ability to learn.

Common Core State Standards Correlations (CCSS)

Correlations have been provided for the Common Core State Standards for Math. For quick viewing of the math correlations, a chart is provided on pages 5 and 6 of this book. (*Note:* This version does not contain page titles but does reference the page numbers.) For a printable PDF version of the correlations chart, go to *www.teachercreated.com/standards/*. These charts correlate student activities to applicable standards within a given domain.

Educators know that children learn in different ways. We know, too, that children need strong math skills to be successful in school. *Instant Math Practice: K* builds on the intuitive and informal math knowledge that students have acquired prior to kindergarten. It provides young learners with a diverse collection of tracing, cutting, fill-in-the-blanks, and puzzle activities with which to explore math skills and concepts. All the pages can be colored for added enjoyment and additional fine-motor development practice.

The skills reviewed in this book are scaffolded (sequential). Begin by introducing the numbers zero through five and later groupings 6–12, 13–20, and 21–30. Students who have accomplished writing numbers and number words should still enjoy the pages and will gather confidence with all they "already know."

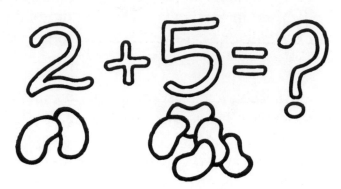

Once students are comfortable with numbers and number amounts, they can progress to arranging sets, identifying shapes and patterns, and computing simple addition and subtraction problems. Pages can be used to reinforce and expand skills in whole- or small-group settings, as support for Response to Intervention (RTI), or for independent practice at home or in class.

Math vocabulary and symbols are foundational to understanding math concepts and doing computations. There are different ways to describe certain math actions, and familiarity with the terms used will allow students to focus on the skill and not the word. Direction words (circle, solve, etc.) are also used throughout the book in page directions. Familiarity with these words will build students' confidence when reading directions for themselves.

Whenever possible, relate the skills being practiced with daily life. Count and sort items and identify patterns and shapes. Make connections—a circle is round, a ball is round, and an orange is round. Look at the numbers on sports jerseys, houses, and license plates. Count snack items, toys as they are put away, and fruits and vegetables while shopping. Notice the shapes of objects in the room and items in nature. Show children that math is used all day, every day, not just in the classroom.

Enjoy this book and help young learners experience numbers in a variety of fun-filled ways!

Common Core State Standards Correlation

Student practice pages in *Instant Math Practice* have been correlated to the following Common Core State Standards © Copyright 2010. National Governors Association Center for Best Practices and Council of Chief State School Officers. All rights reserved.

For more information about the Common Core State Standards, go to *http://www.corestandards.org/*.

Mathematics Standards	Page
Counting & Cardinality	
Know number names and the count sequence.	
K.CC.1. Count to 100 by ones and by tens.	14, 15, 21, 22, 25, 26, 27, 35, 36, 44, 45, 46, 50, 51, 52, 53, 54, 55, 56, 57, 62, 63, 69, 70
K.CC.2. Count forward beginning from a given number within the known sequence (instead of having to begin at 1).	34, 60, 65, 66
K.CC.3. Write numbers from 0 to 20. Represent a number of objects with a written numeral 0–20 (with 0 representing a count of no objects).	7, 8, 9, 10, 11, 12, 14, 18, 21, 23, 24, 25, 26, 27, 28, 29, 30, 31, 35, 36, 37, 38, 39, 40, 41, 42, 43, 48, 49, 52, 53, 54, 55, 56, 57, 58, 60, 62
Count to tell the number of objects.	
K.CC.4. Understand the relationship between numbers and quantities; connect counting to cardinality.	13, 14, 15, 16, 17, 20, 21, 22, 23, 28, 30, 31, 34, 35, 36, 45, 46, 48, 49, 50, 51, 53, 54, 55, 58, 59, 61, 62, 63, 67, 68
K.CC.4a. When counting objects, say the number names in the standard order, pairing each object with one and only one number name and each number name with one and only one object.	13, 16, 21, 22, 31, 35, 36, 45, 54, 55, 56, 57, 63
K.CC.4b. Understand that the last number name said tells the number of objects counted. The number of objects is the same regardless of their arrangement or the order in which they were counted.	14, 15, 16, 20, 21, 22, 28, 31, 32, 35, 36, 45, 48, 49, 54, 55, 61, 62, 63
K.CC.4c. Understand that each successive number name refers to a quantity that is one larger.	14, 16, 17, 28, 30, 34, 44, 60
K.CC.5. Count to answer "how many?" questions about as many as 20 things arranged in a line, a rectangular array, or a circle, or as many as 10 things in a scattered configuration; given a number from 1–20, count out that many objects.	14, 15, 21, 22, 26, 27, 28, 35, 36, 45, 46, 48, 49, 50, 51, 52, 53, 55, 56, 57, 61, 62
Compare numbers.	
K.CC.6. Identify whether the number of objects in one group is greater than, less than, or equal to the number of objects in another group, e.g., by using matching and counting strategies.	19, 20, 27, 31, 32, 33, 34, 58, 59, 89
K.CC.7. Compare two numbers between 1 and 10 presented as written numerals.	31, 34

Operations & Algebraic Thinking	
Understand addition, and understand subtraction.	
K.OA.1. Represent addition and subtraction with objects, fingers, mental images, drawings, sounds (e.g., claps), acting out situations, verbal explanations, expressions, or equations.	29, 71, 72, 73, 74, 76, 77, 78, 79, 80, 81, 82, 83, 85, 86, 87, 88, 89, 92, 93, 94, 95, 96, 97, 98, 99, 100, 101, 102, 104, 105, 106, 107, 108, 109, 110, 111, 113, 114, 115, 118, 119, 120, 121, 122, 123, 124, 125, 126, 128, 129, 130, 131, 132, 133, 134, 135, 136
K.OA.2. Solve addition and subtraction word problems, and add and subtract within 10, e.g., by using objects or drawings to represent the problem.	29, 75, 77, 78, 84, 88, 90, 91, 92, 93, 96, 99, 103, 112, 116, 117, 124, 127
K.OA.3. Decompose numbers less than or equal to 10 into pairs in more than one way, e.g., by using objects or drawings, and record each decomposition by a drawing or equation (e.g., $5 = 2 + 3$ and $5 = 4 + 1$).	71, 72, 73, 74, 76, 77, 79, 80, 85, 86, 88, 89, 131, 132
K.OA.5. Fluently add and subtract within 5.	29, 71, 72, 73, 74, 75, 104, 105, 106, 107, 108
Number & Operations in Base Ten	
Work with numbers 11–19 to gain foundations for place value.	
K.NBT.1. Compose and decompose numbers from 11 to 19 into ten ones and some further ones, e.g., by using objects or drawings, and record each composition or decomposition by a drawing or equation (such as $18 = 10 + 8$); understand that these numbers are composed of ten ones and one, two, three, four, five, six, seven, eight, or nine ones.	67, 68, 69, 70
Measurement & Data	
Classify objects and count the number of objects in each category.	
K.MD.3. Classify objects into given categories; count the numbers of objects in each category and sort the categories by count.	18, 19, 21, 22, 23, 24, 32, 35, 36, 48, 49, 56, 57, 74, 81, 87, 94, 95, 112, 122
Geometry	
Analyze, compare, create, and compose shapes.	
K.G.5. Model shapes in the world by building shapes from components (e.g., sticks and clay balls) and drawing shapes.	28, 29, 54, 55, 73, 84

Time to Eat

Count the fish and the bears. Write the amount in the box near each set. Draw a line from the fish on the left to the matching set of bears in the column on the right.

Equal Sets 0–5

Sort the Sets

Cut out the animals. Sort the animals into two equal sets. Place the fish in the water and the frogs on land or on the log.

High-Flying Numbers

Count the dots on each kite. Circle each dot as you count it. Draw a string from each kite to the correct number.

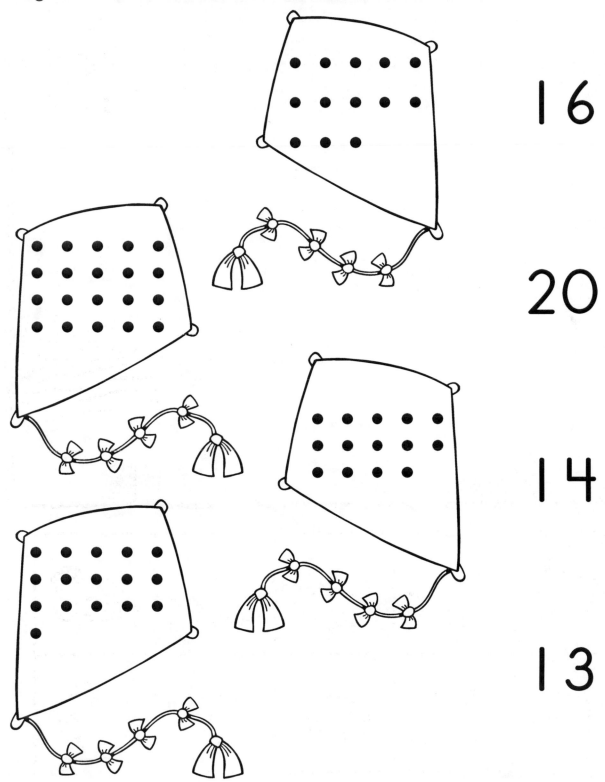

16

20

14

13

Color the Numbers 13–20

Hatching Answers

Use the numbers in the Color Code to color the picture.

Color Code	13 = blue	15 = green	17 = orange	19 = purple
	14 = yellow	16 = brown	18 = black	20 = red

Count the Stars

Write the number in the box below the number word. Circle the correct number of stars in each group to match the number.

thirty

twenty-two

twenty-nine

twenty-five

So Many Shapes

Count the shapes in each row. Circle the total in the box at the end of the row.

1	20 21 22

2	28 29 30

3	26 27 28

4	21 22 23

Tens and Ones

Circle each group of ten. Count the remaining ones. Write the totals on the lines below.

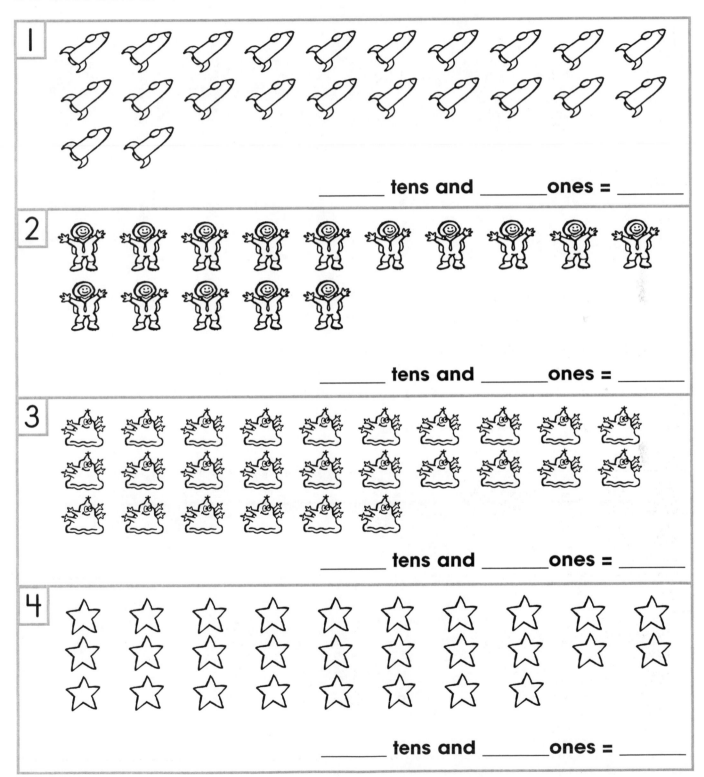

1. _____ tens and _____ ones = _____

2. _____ tens and _____ ones = _____

3. _____ tens and _____ ones = _____

4. _____ tens and _____ ones = _____

More Tens and Ones

Circle each group of ten. Count the remaining ones. Write the totals on the lines below.

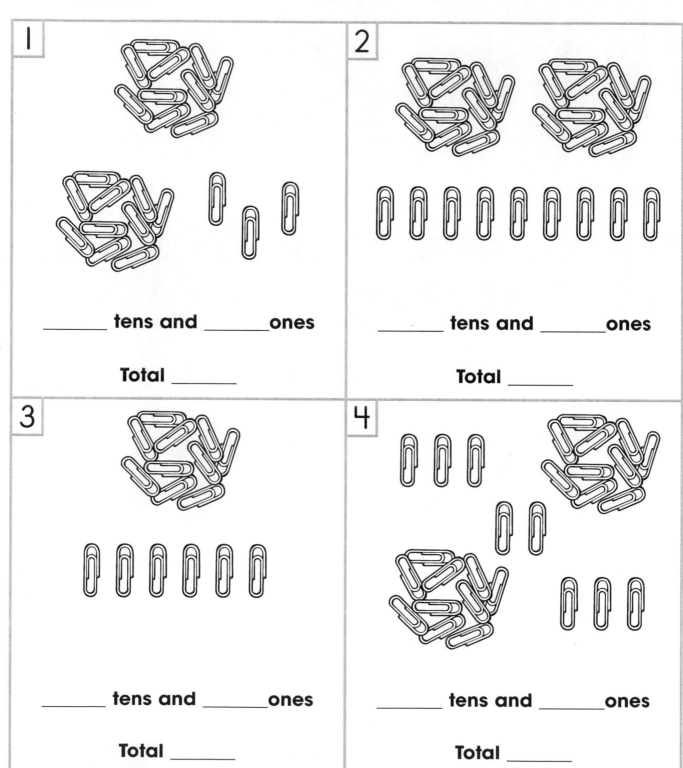

1

_____ tens and _____ones

Total _____

2

_____ tens and _____ones

Total _____

3

_____ tens and _____ones

Total _____

4

_____ tens and _____ones

Total _____

Addition 0–5

Adding Animals

Count the animals in each set. Add the sets together. How many animals in all?

1

_____ + _____ = _____

2

_____ + _____ = _____

3
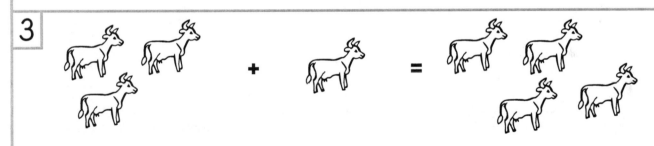

_____ + _____ = _____

4

_____ + _____ = _____

Addition 0–5

Sailboats at Sea

Write an addition sentence for each set of pictures.

1

_____ + _____ = _____

2

_____ + _____ = _____

3

_____ + _____ = _____

Addition 0–5

Shape Sets

Look at each number problem and the shape it is in. Draw shapes for each set. Find the sums. The first one has been done for you.

◇ 1 + 4	 + 	= ◇ 5
▭ 3 + 2		= ▭
△ 4 + 1		= △
◯ 2 + 2		= ◯
□ 2 + 1		= □

Fill the Basket

Solve the problems. Paste the fruits that have sums that equal 5 in the basket.

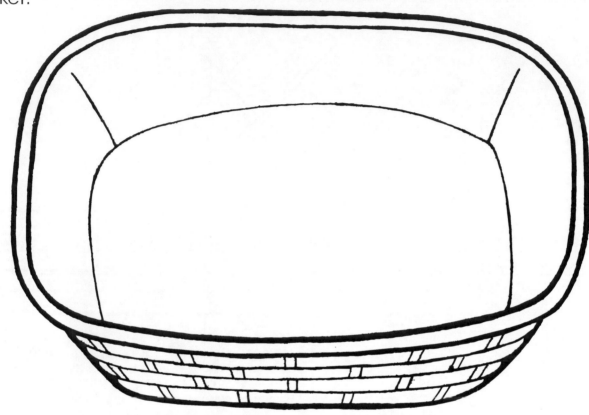

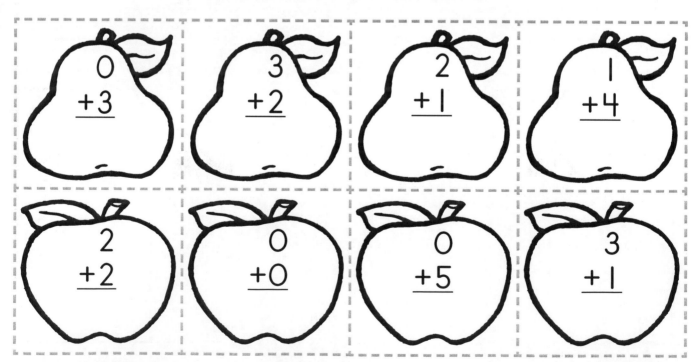

Hide and Seek

Read and solve the word problems.

1

Two gray mice hopped in the hay.

Two more came over to play.

How many mice played that day?

_____ + _____ = _____

2

Three green frogs sat on a log.

Two more frogs hopped out of the fog.

How many frogs croaked in the bog?

_____ + _____ = _____

3

Two orange cats sat.

One more came wearing a hat.

How many cats are now on the mat?

_____ + _____ = _____

Count and Add

Write an addition sentence for each set of pictures.

1

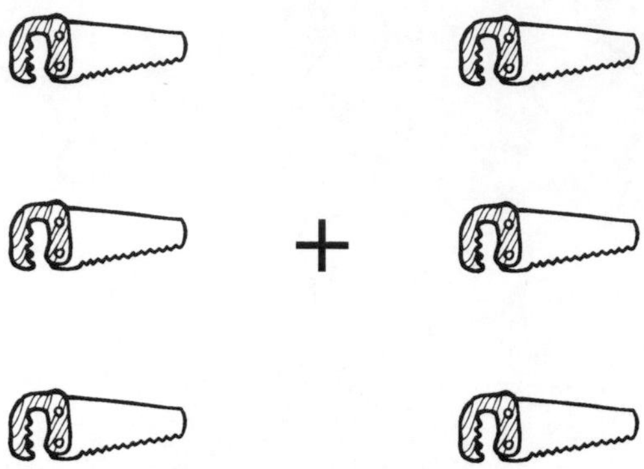

_____ + _____ = _____

2

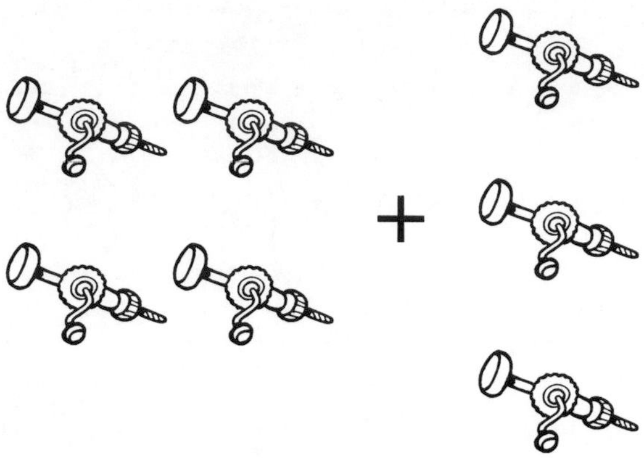

_____ + _____ = _____

3

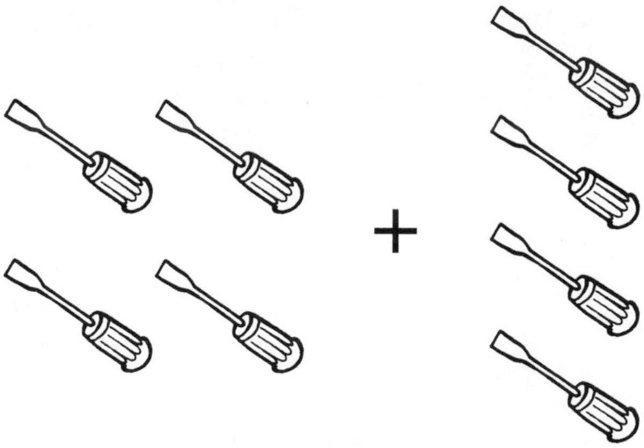

_____ + _____ = _____

4

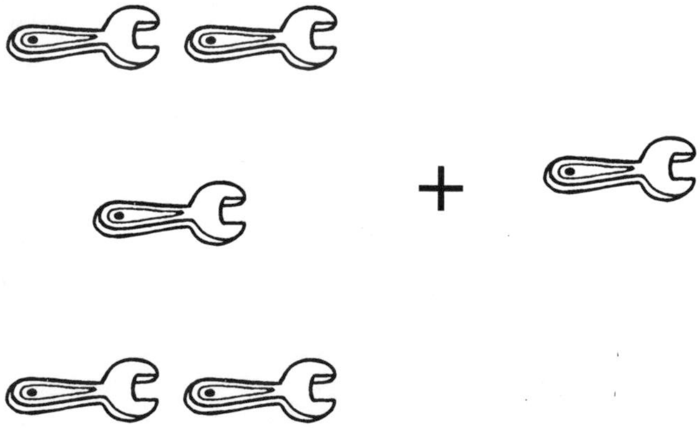

_____ + _____ = _____

Add the Dinosaurs

Count the different sets of dinosaurs in each picture. Solve the problems.

Frogs at Play

Solve the problems. Then follow the directions below the frogs.

1. Color the frog that had the missing number 5 green.
2. Color the frog that had the missing number 4 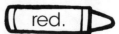 red.
3. Color the frog that had the missing number 7 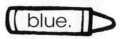 blue.
4. Color the frog that had the missing number 0  yellow.
5. Color the frog that had the missing number 2  orange.

School Supplies

Count the school supplies in each box. Add the items to find the total.

1	2
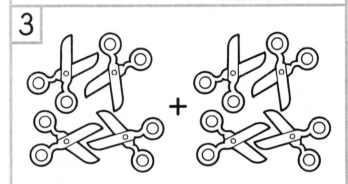	
6 + 3 = ___	4 + 3 = ___

3	4
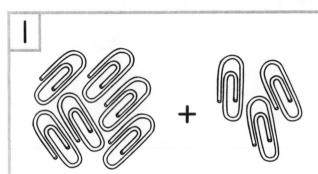	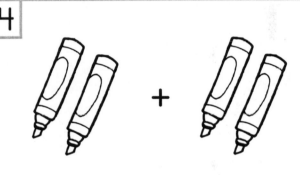
4 + 4 = ___	2 + 2 = ___

5	6
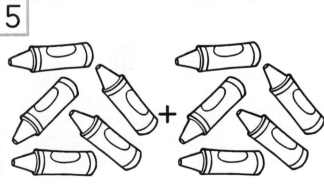	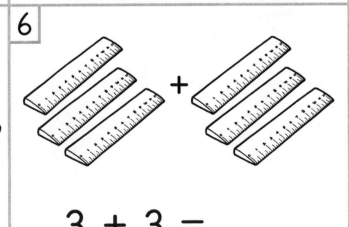
5 + 5 = ___	3 + 3 = ___

Addition 0–10

How Many Pets?

Count the pets in each set and write the numbers underneath. Solve the problem. Write the total on each pet home.

_____ + _____ = _____

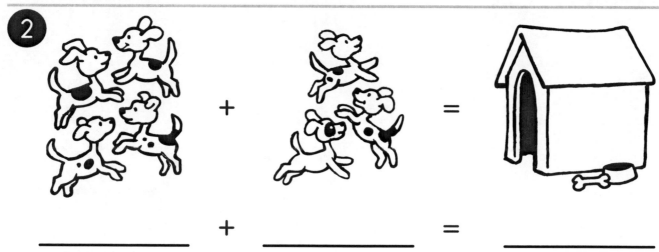

_____ + _____ = _____

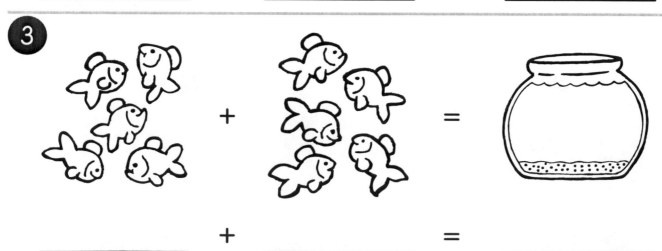

_____ + _____ = _____

Digging for Answers

Solve the problem in each bone. Find the bones with sums that are odd.
Color those bones brown.

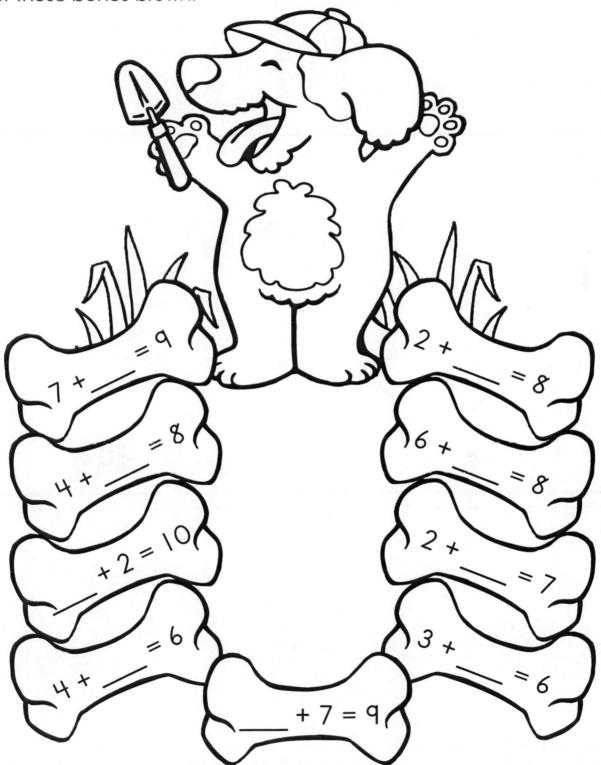

7 + _____ = 9

4 + _____ = 8

_____ + 2 = 10

4 + _____ = 6

_____ + 7 = 9

2 + _____ = 8

6 + _____ = 8

2 + _____ = 7

3 + _____ = 6

Fishing Fun

Solve the problem on each fish. Draw a fishing line from the rod to the fish that has the **greatest** sum.

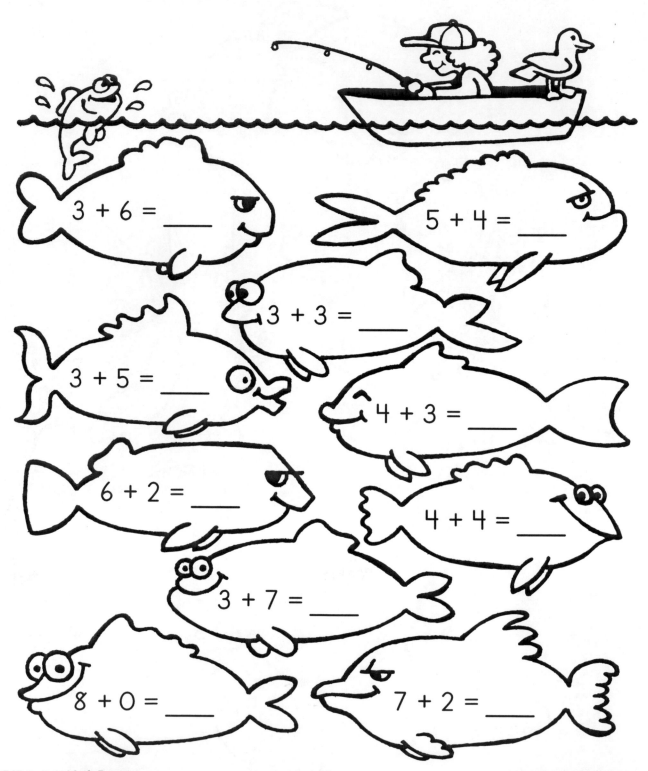

$3 + 6 =$ ___

$5 + 4 =$ ___

$3 + 3 =$ ___

$3 + 5 =$ ___

$4 + 3 =$ ___

$6 + 2 =$ ___

$4 + 4 =$ ___

$3 + 7 =$ ___

$8 + 0 =$ ___

$7 + 2 =$ ___

Solve the Mystery

Solve the problems. Each time you use a number, color that number in the treasure chest. The mystery number will be the one that is not colored.

$4 + \underline{\hspace{1.5cm}} = 9$

$\underline{\hspace{1.5cm}} + 2 = 10$

$3 + \underline{\hspace{1.5cm}} = 5$

$\underline{\hspace{1.5cm}} + 8 = 8$

$1 + \underline{\hspace{1.5cm}} = 2$

$2 + \underline{\hspace{1.5cm}} = 8$

$\underline{\hspace{1.5cm}} + 1 = 4$

$3 + \underline{\hspace{1.5cm}} = 10$

$\underline{\hspace{1.5cm}} + 2 = 6$

What is the mystery number?

Shape Word Problems

Read and solve the word problems. Draw the shapes to show your work.

| 1 | Sam has 6 triangles and Jan has 3 triangles. How many triangles do they have all together? | 6
+ 3 ——— |

| 2 | Pam has 5 circles and Jack has 5 circles. How many circles do they have all together? | + ——— |

| 3 | Sally has 4 rectangles and Li has 2 rectangles. How many rectangles do they have all together? | + ——— |

| 4 | Jose has 7 squares and Ani has 2 squares. How many squares do they have all together? |  |

| 5 | Draw and solve a shape problem of your own. |  |

Add Them Up!

Count the items in each set. Write and solve the addition problems.

1

_____ + _____ = _____

2

+ = _____

3

_____ + _____ = _____

4

_____ + _____ = _____

5

_____ + _____ = _____

Domino Dot Addition

Write an addition sentence for each domino.

1 _____ + _____ = _____

2 _____ + _____ = _____

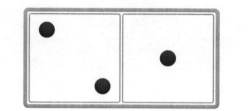

3 _____ + _____ = _____

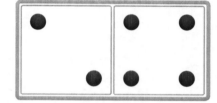

4 _____ + _____ = _____

5 _____ + _____ = _____

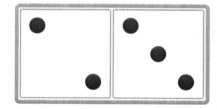

6 _____ + _____ = _____

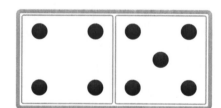

Solve the problems. Draw the missing dots on the dominoes.

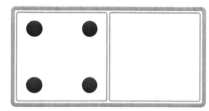

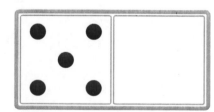

7 4 + _____ = 5   **8** 2 + _____ = 8   **9** 5 + _____ = 9

Hanging Out

Solve each problem. Color the items with answers that are **odd** numbers.

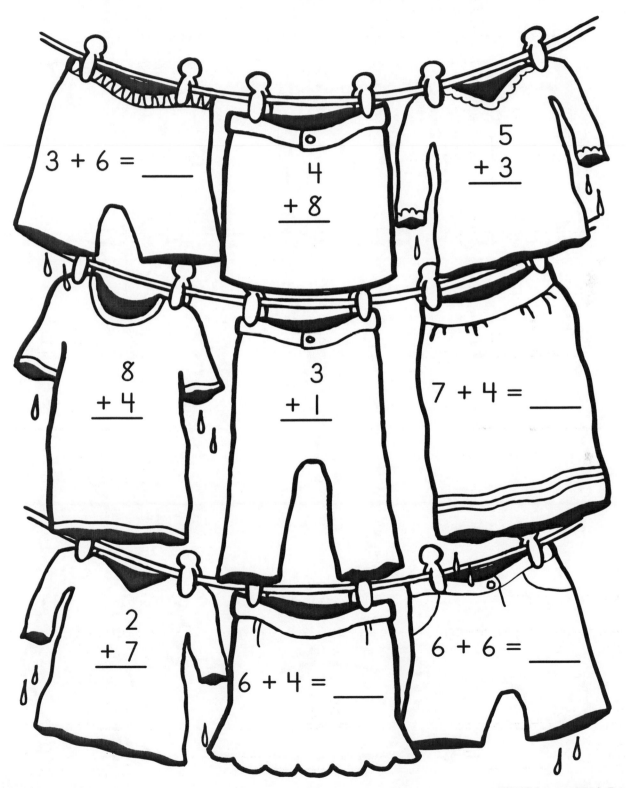

3 + 6 = _____

4
+ 8
___

5
+ 3
___

8
+ 4
___

3
+ 1
___

7 + 4 = _____

2
+ 7
___

6 + 4 = _____

6 + 6 = _____

Farmyard Facts

Solve the problems. Follow the directions for each row.

1 Color the feed sacks that have sums that equal 12.

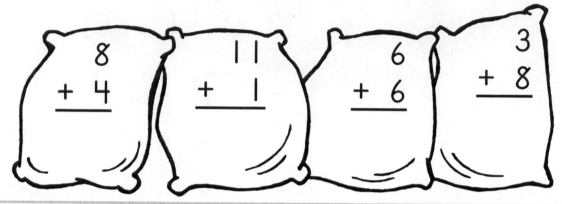

$$8 + 4$$ $$11 + 1$$ $$6 + 6$$ $$3 + 8$$

2 Color the hay bales that have sums that equal 9.

3 + 9 = ___   2 + 6 = ___

4 + 5 = ___   7 + 2 = ___

3 Color the hens that have sums that equal 12.

13 + 2 = ___ $$12 + 0$$

7 + 5 = ___

Addition 0–12

More for Lunch

Find the sum of the items in each lunchbox. Circle the lunchbox in each row with the larger sum.

$8 + 3 = $ _____

$1 + 7 = $ _____

$2 + 6 = $ _____

$6 + 6 = $ _____

$9 + 2 = $ _____

$8 + 0 = $ _____

Addition 0–15

Add the Beans

Color the beans using the code on the right. Some will be left white.
Answer the questions and solve the problems at the bottom.

Color Code
1 purple bean
2 brown beans
3 red beans
4 pink beans
5 orange beans
6 green beans
7 yellow beans
8 black beans
9 blue beans

1. How many beans are white? _____

2. How many beans are red or green? _____ + _____ = _____

3. How many beans are red or blue? _____ + _____ = _____

4. How many beans are pink or red? _____ + _____ = _____

5. How many beans are orange or green? _____ + _____ = _____

6. How many beans are yellow or black? _____ + _____ = _____

7. How many beans are pink or blue? _____ + _____ = _____

Fill the Jars

Follow the directions for each problem. Then write the missing number.

1 Draw 12 beans in the jar.
Color eight beans red.
Color the other beans yellow.
Complete the addition sentence.

$8 +$ _____ $= 12$

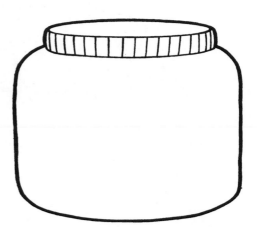

2 Draw 11 beans in the jar.
Color seven beans blue.
Color the other beans orange.
Complete the addition sentence.

$7 +$ _____ $= 11$

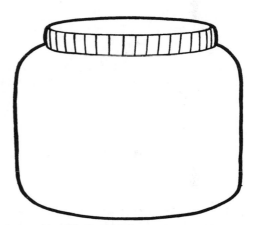

3 Draw 15 beans in the jar.
Color six beans purple.
Color the other beans green.
Complete the addition sentence.

$6 +$ _____ $= 15$

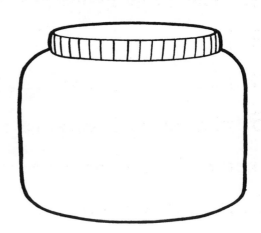

Addition 0–15

Surprise!

Solve the problems. Write the letter that matches the sum in the box below the problem. Read the words to see what is in the lunchbox.

11	12	13	14	15
r	g	a	o	f

8	9	4	14	8
+ 5	+ 6	+ 7	+ 0	+ 4

Pack Full of Money

One of these backpacks is filled with money. Solve each problem. Then follow the directions below. Circle the lucky backpack.

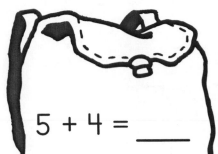

$5 + 4 =$ ____

$\begin{array}{r} 6 \\ + 7 \\ \hline \end{array}$

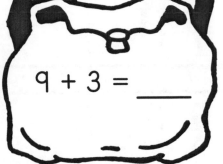

$5 + 3 =$ ____

$8 + 3 =$ ____

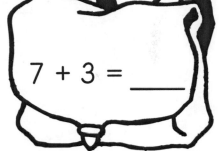

$5 + 10 =$ ____

$7 + 3 =$ ____

$2 + 5 =$ ____

$7 + 7 =$ ____

$9 + 3 =$ ____

It is not 11. Cross it out.

It is not 8. Cross it out.

It is not 9. Cross it out.

It is not 12. Cross it out.

It is not 14. Cross it out.

It is not 15. Cross it out.

It is not 13. Cross it out.

It is not 7. Cross it out.

Are They Ripe?

Solve the problems. The oranges with the **odd** number sums are ripe.

How many oranges are ripe? ☐

Batter Up!

Solve the problems in each ball. **Even** number sums are home runs. How many home runs were scored in the game?

Smell the Flowers

The answer to each problem is in the center of the flower. Fill in the blanks to solve the problems.

Addition 0–20

Brick by Brick

Solve the problem in each brick. If the answer is an **odd** number, color the brick red.

$15 + 4 =$

$6 + 3 =$

$12 + 2 =$ $10 + 10 =$

$4 + 8 =$

$5 + 9 =$ $2 + 7 =$

$6 + 5 =$

$3 + 8 =$ $10 + 4 =$

$9 + 10 =$

$6 + 8 =$ $7 + 10 =$

$9 + 3 =$

$12 + 5 =$ $3 + 17 =$

$9 + 7 =$

Break the Code

Fill in the missing numbers to solve the problems. Use the letter code to solve the secret message.

1 $2 + \underline{} = 11$
o

2 $3 + \underline{} = 6$
u

3 $5 + \underline{} = 9$
r

4 $2 + \underline{} = 14$
p

5 $7 + \underline{} = 17$
s

6 $8 + \underline{} = 13$
f

7 $4 + \underline{} = 12$
e

8 $3 + \underline{} = 10$
l

9 $12 + \underline{} = 18$
v

10 $4 + \underline{} = 6$
n

11 $8 + \underline{} = 8$
q

12 $19 + \underline{} = 20$
a

Secret Message

$\underline{}$ $\underline{}$ $\underline{}$ $\underline{}$ $\underline{}$ $\underline{}$ $\underline{}$ $\underline{}$
5   9   3   4   12   7   3   10

$\underline{}$ $\underline{}$ $\underline{}$ $\underline{}$ $\underline{}$
10   8   6   8   2

$\underline{}$ $\underline{}$ $\underline{}$ $\underline{}$ $\underline{}$ $\underline{}$
8   0   3   1   7   10

$\underline{}$ $\underline{}$ $\underline{}$ $\underline{}$ $\underline{}$ $\underline{}$
8   7   8   6   8   2

Rewrite the message as a number sentence. $\underline{} + \underline{} = \underline{}$

Cookie Count

1 There was a tray of 20 cookies for the party. There were 10 boys and 10 girls at the party.

Was there a cookie for each child at the party? YES   NO

_____ + _____ = _____

2 Randy, Leslie, and Sam each had four cookies after school. How many cookies did they eat all together? Draw cookies to show your work.

_____ + _____ + _____ = _____

Grab That Ball!

Find the sum in each football. Color the footballs with sums **greater than** twenty.

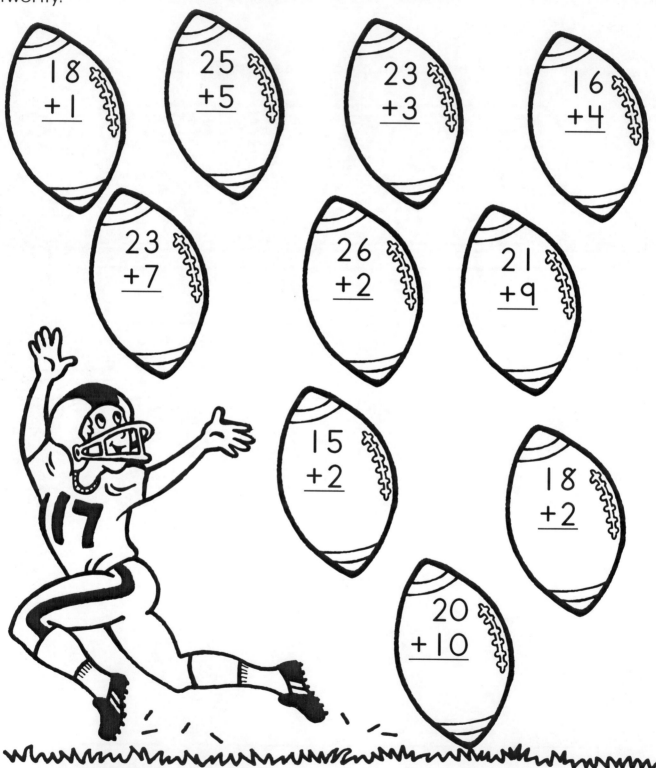

18
+1

25
+5

23
+3

16
+4

23
+7

26
+2

21
+9

15
+2

18
+2

20
+10

Addition 0–30

The Big Peanut Search

Elephant likes to eat peanuts. He is looking for the peanut with the **largest** number for an answer. Solve the problems and circle the peanut with the largest answer.

20 + 4 = _____

13 + 7 = _____

8 + 6 = _____

17 + 4 = _____

10 + 8 = _____

15 + 6 = _____

23 + 5 = _____

10 + 5 = _____

25 + 3 = _____

13 + 8 = _____

20 + 9 = _____

Grapes Are Great!

Find the sum in each grape. Color each grape with a total of nineteen purple. Color each grape with a total less than nineteen green. Color the grapes with sums greater than nineteen red.

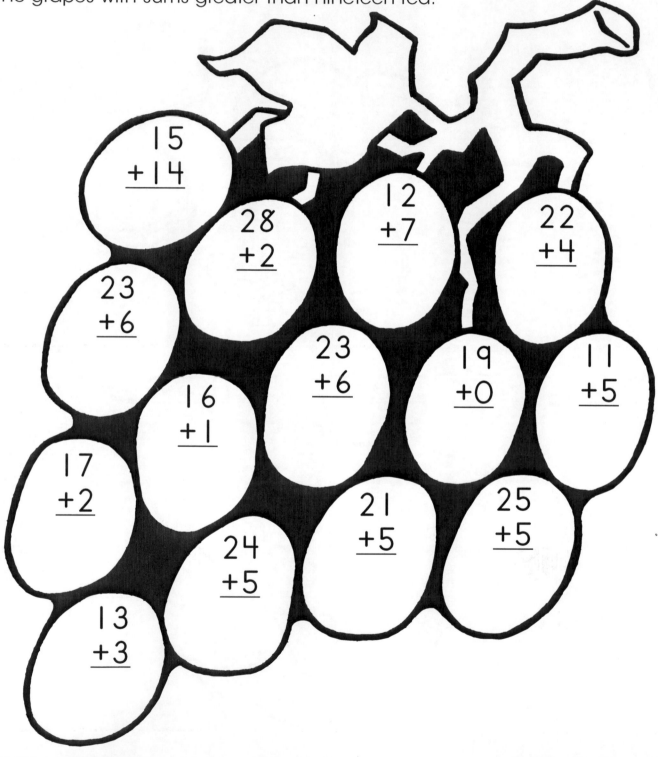

Word Problems

Read and solve each word problem. Show your work.

1

Everyone was getting off the bus. Nine players got off the bus. Ten parents got off the bus. How many people got off the bus?

2

There were many bikes in the racks at school. There were 10 red bikes, 10 blue bikes and six green bikes. How many bikes were there all together?

3

Mary and Erica put all their crayons in a box. Mary had nine crayons and Erica had 20 crayons. How many crayons were in the box?

4

All the animals got out of the barn. There were 11 horses, nine cows, and two pigs running around the field. How many animals got out of the barn?

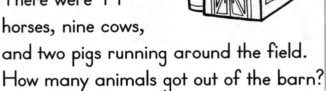
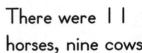

Bouncing Back

Subtraction is the opposite of addition. Instead of adding to a number, an amount is taken away. Look at each problem. Mark the number of hops back the kangaroo will take to solve the problem. The first one has been done for you.

1 5 – 2 = _3_

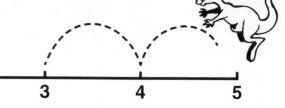

0	1	2	3	4	5

2 5 – 3 = ____

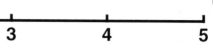

0	1	2	3	4	5

3 5 – 4 = ____

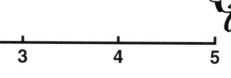

0	1	2	3	4	5

4 5 – 0 = ____

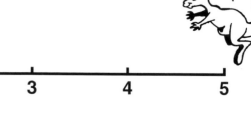

0	1	2	3	4	5

5 5 – 1 = ____

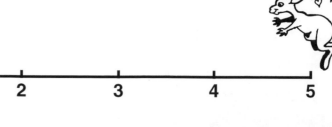

0	1	2	3	4	5

Bears Over the Mountain

Count all the bears at each mountain. Look on the right side of the mountain to see how many bears have walked away. Write a subtraction problem for the bears on each mountain.

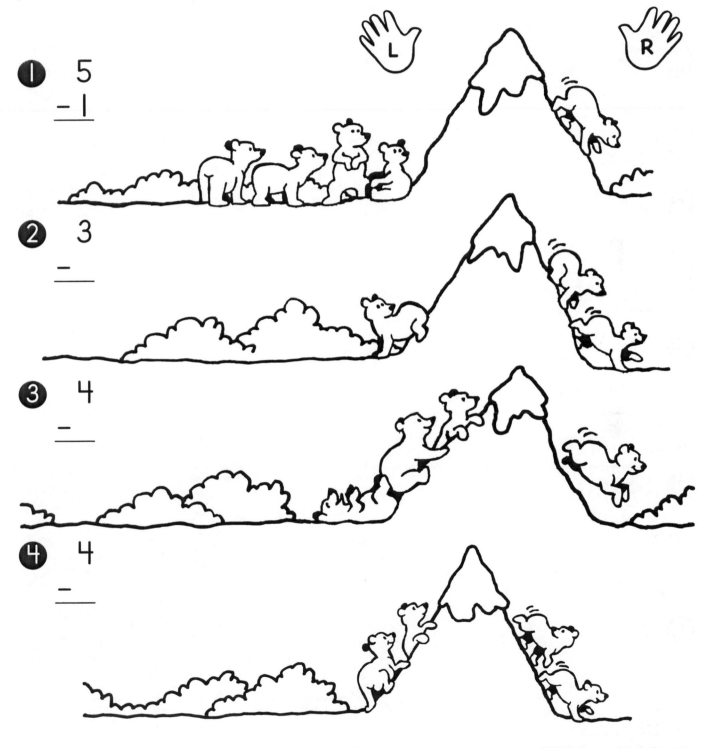

1 5
   – 1

2 3
   –

3 4
   –

4 4
   –

How Many Monkeys?

Solve each subtraction problem on the left. The answer will be the number of monkeys still jumping on the bed. Draw a line from the answer to the correct picture on the right.

1 5
   −2

2 5
   −4

3 5
   −1

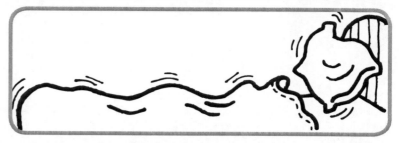

4 5
   −3

5 5
   −5

Domino Dot Subtraction

How many more dots does one side have than the other? Write a subtraction problem for each domino. The first one has been done for you.

1 $\underline{\ \ 4\ \ } - \underline{\ \ 1\ \ } = \underline{\ \ 3\ \ }$

5 $\underline{\quad} - \underline{\quad} = \underline{\quad}$

2 $\underline{\quad} - \underline{\quad} = \underline{\quad}$

6 $\underline{\quad} - \underline{\quad} = \underline{\quad}$

3 $\underline{\quad} - \underline{\quad} = \underline{\quad}$

7 $\underline{\quad} - \underline{\quad} = \underline{\quad}$

4 $\underline{\quad} - \underline{\quad} = \underline{\quad}$

8 $\underline{\quad} - \underline{\quad} = \underline{\quad}$

Play Ball

Do the subtraction problems first. Then use the code to find the answers to the questions.

Code
0 = c
1 = a
2 = b
3 = t

① What animal loves to play baseball?

5 – 3 = _____   4 – 3 = _____   3 – 0 = _____

Answer: _____ _____ _____

② What animal makes a good catcher?

3 – 3 = _____   2 – 1 = _____   3 – 0 = _____

Answer: _____ _____ _____

③ What will the cat and the bat take after the game?

2 – 2 = _____   1 – 0 = _____   4 – 2 = _____

Answer: _____ _____ _____

More Domino Dots

Finish the subtraction sentences. Then write the problems using the symbol for subtraction.

1

6 dots take away _____ dots equals _____ dots

____ ____ = ____

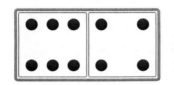

2

6 dots take away _____ dots equals _____ dots

____ ____ = ____

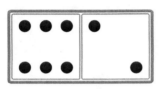

3

6 dots take away _____ dots equals _____ dots

____ ____ = ____

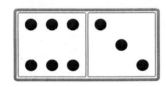

4

6 dots take away _____ dots equals _____ dot

____ ____ = ____

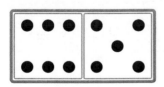

5

6 dots take away _____ dots equals _____ dots

____ ____ = ____

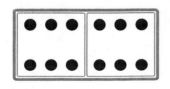

Subtraction 0–8

How Many Are Left?

Count the items in each box. Subtract the number crossed out.
Complete the problems.

1

$6 - 2 =$ _____

2

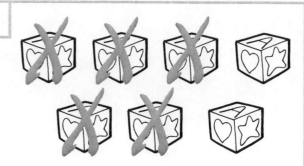

$7 - 5 =$ _____

3

$8 - 3 =$ _____

4

$6 - 1 =$ _____

5

$5 - 1 =$ _____

6

$4 - 0 =$ _____

Make the Team

Each bug team needs nine players. Look at each picture and count how many players they have. Subtract that number from nine to figure out how many more they need.

	Have	Need

1

9 – _____ = _____

2

9 – _____ = _____

3

9 – _____ = _____

4

9 – _____ = _____

5

9 – _____ = _____

6

9 – _____ = _____

Graph to Solve

Count each kind of bug. Fill in the squares to match the count. Use the graph to solve each subtraction problem.

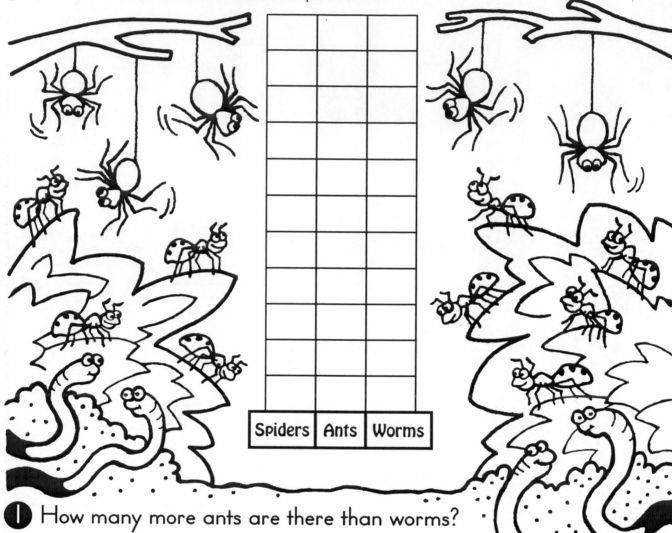

| Spiders | Ants | Worms |

1 How many more ants are there than worms?

_____ - _____ = _____

2 How many more ants are there than spiders?

_____ - _____ = _____

3 How many more worms are there than spiders?

_____ - _____ = _____

See How They Float

Write a subtraction sentence for each picture.

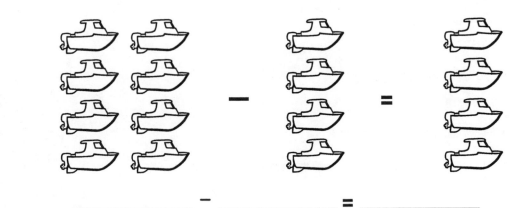

Play Ball

Solve the problem in each bat on the left. Draw a line from the bat to a mitt and ball on the right with the correct answer.

1 10 − 3 = _____

2 8 − 4 = _____

3 5 − 2 = _____

4 9 − 5 = _____

5 7 − 4 = _____

6 6 − 5 = _____

 4

 3

 7

 3

 1

 4

Subtraction Rainbow

Complete each subtraction problem. Then use the Color Code to color the picture.

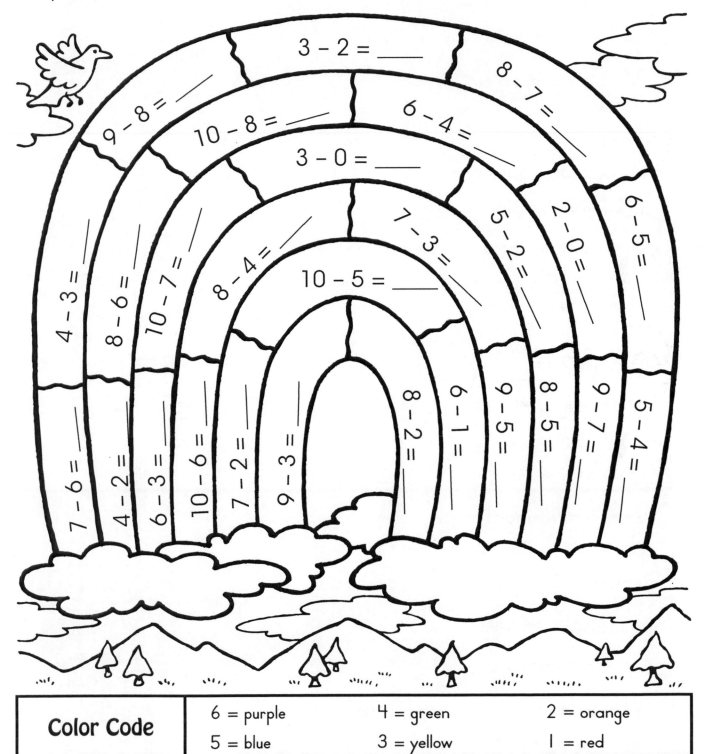

Color Code	6 = purple	4 = green	2 = orange
	5 = blue	3 = yellow	1 = red

Subtraction Word Problems 0–10

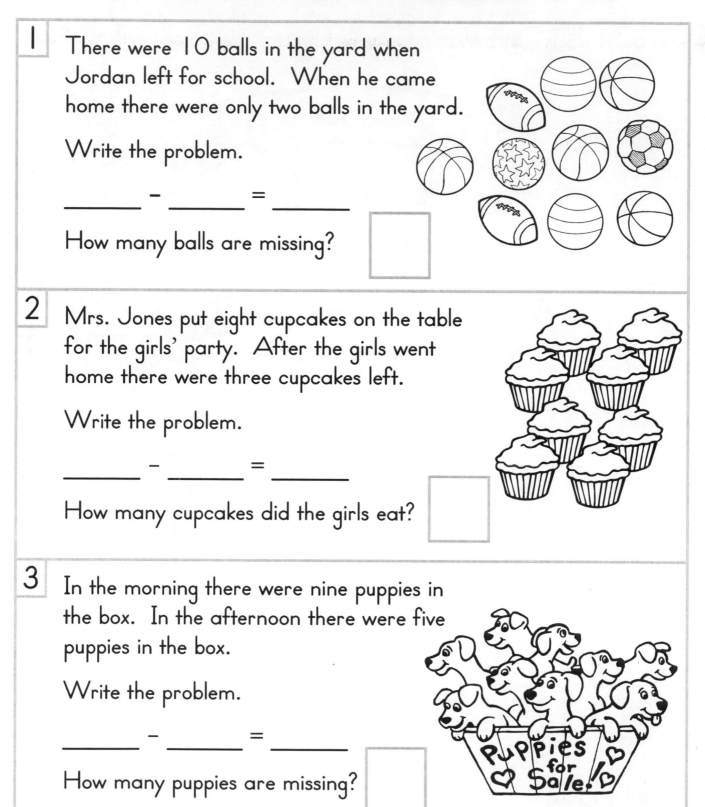

1 There were 10 balls in the yard when Jordan left for school. When he came home there were only two balls in the yard.

Write the problem.

_____ – _____ = _____

How many balls are missing?

2 Mrs. Jones put eight cupcakes on the table for the girls' party. After the girls went home there were three cupcakes left.

Write the problem.

_____ – _____ = _____

How many cupcakes did the girls eat?

3 In the morning there were nine puppies in the box. In the afternoon there were five puppies in the box.

Write the problem.

_____ – _____ = _____

How many puppies are missing?

Subtraction 0–12

Hop Down the Line

Hop backwards on the number line to subtract. Help Freddy Frog figure out how many more hops he needs to get to his log.

1 How many hops did Freddy Frog hop? _____

How many more hops does he need to get to the log? _____

12 – ____ = ____

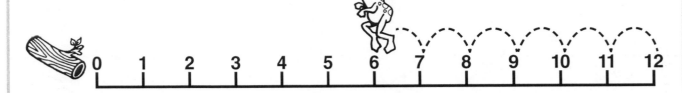

2 How many hops did Freddy Frog hop? _____

How many more hops does he need to get to the log? _____

12 – ____ = ____

3 How many hops did Freddy Frog hop? _____

How many more hops does he need to get to the log? _____

12 – ____ = ____

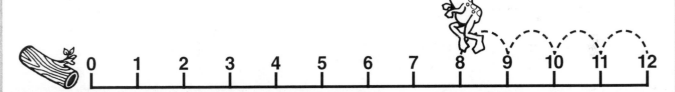

Subtraction 0–12

Let's Go!

Count the vehicles in each box. Read the problem below it. Cross out the vehicles taken away. Solve the problems.

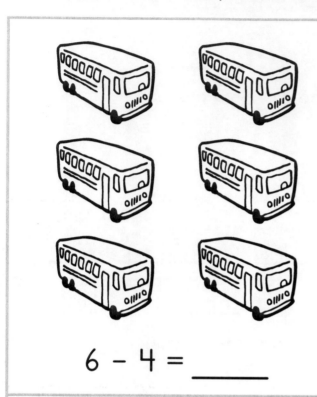

6 – 4 = _____

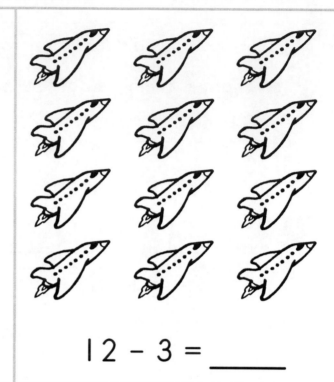

12 – 3 = _____

8 – 5 = _____

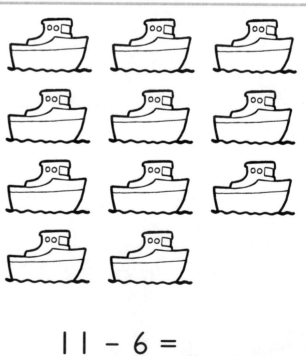

11 – 6 = _____

Missing Clothes

Look at the problem. Cross out the items to be subtracted. Solve the problem.

1

$12 - 6 = $ _____

2

$9 - 5 = $ _____

3

$10 - 5 = $ _____

4

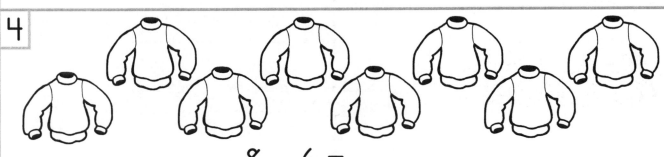

$8 - 6 = $ _____

A Dozen or Less

Look at each egg carton. Write a subtraction problem for each carton on the left. Rewrite the problem on the right. The first one has been done for you.

1

$12 - \underline{5} = \underline{7}$

$$\begin{array}{r} 12 \\ -\ 5 \\ \hline 7 \end{array}$$

2

$12 - \underline{} = \underline{}$

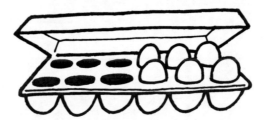

$$\begin{array}{r} 12 \\ -\ \\ \hline \end{array}$$

3

$12 - \underline{} = \underline{}$

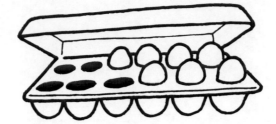

$$\begin{array}{r} 12 \\ -\ \\ \hline \end{array}$$

4

$12 - \underline{} = \underline{}$

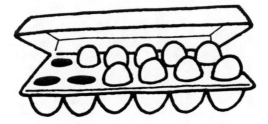

$$\begin{array}{r} 12 \\ -\ \\ \hline \end{array}$$

5

$12 - \underline{} = \underline{}$

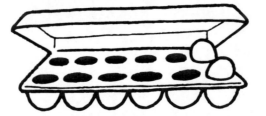

$$\begin{array}{r} 12 \\ -\ \\ \hline \end{array}$$

Subtraction 0–12

Ducks on the Run!

Solve each subtraction problem. Use the code to write the correct letter under each answer to find out where the ducks are going.

Code

1	=	w
2	=	i
3	=	n
4	=	m
5	=	s
6	=	g

```
  10      8      6     12     10      9     11     12
 - 5    - 7    - 4    - 8    - 6    - 7    - 8    - 6
 ----   ----   ----   ----   ----   ----   ----   ----
```

____   ____   ____   ____   ____   ____   ____   ____

Subtraction 0–20

Turtle Talk

Solve the subtraction problems. Color the sections with **even** number answers orange. Color the **odd** number answers green.

122

Taking Off

Many balloons were in the air. Some landed. Subtract the number of balloons on the ground from the total number of balloons in each box.

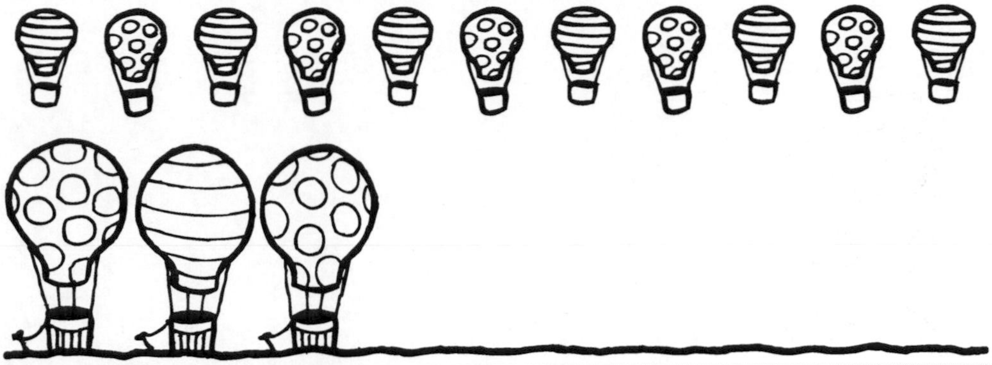

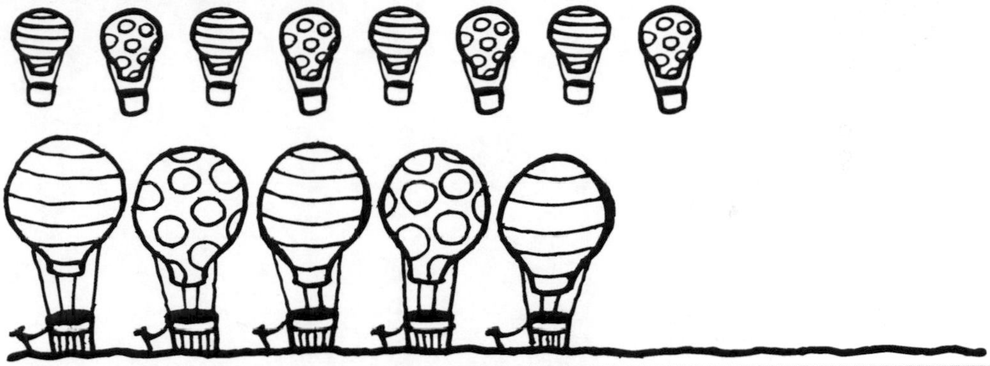

1 14
   – ___

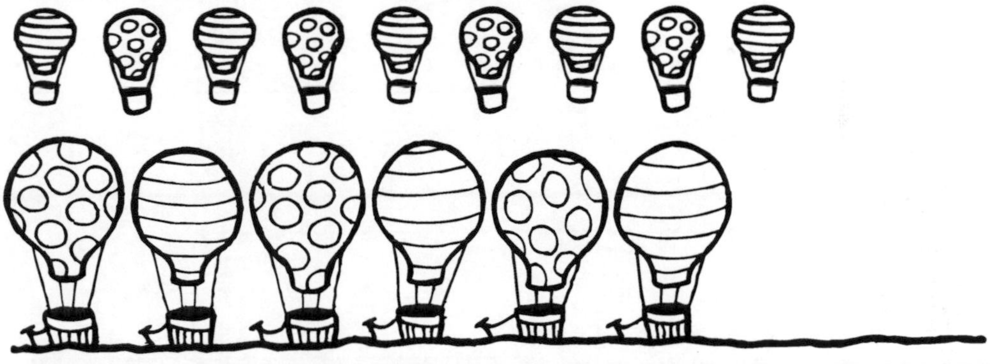

2 13
   – ___

3 15
   – ___

4 12
   – ___

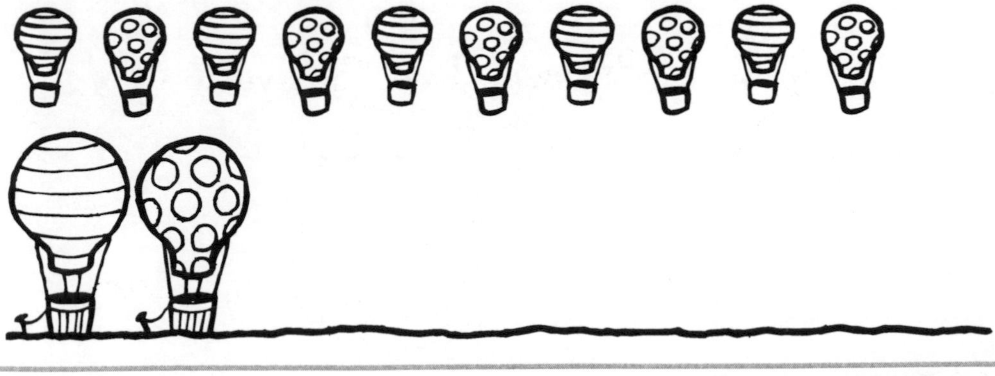

A Sneaky Snake

Solve the problems. Then fill in the number code to see what the sneaky snake has to say.

15 – 10 = _____ G   17 – 6 = _____ R

20 – 19 = _____ A   13 – 6 = _____ K

20 – 8 = _____ S   14 – 11 = _____ C

17 – 15 = _____ B   17 – 9 = _____ L

20 – 11 = _____ N   12 – 6 = _____ H

16 – 12 = _____ E   13 – 3 = _____ O

❶ I can strike hard with my _____ _____ _____ _____, but I
   do not bite.   9   10   12   4

❷ I can _____ _____ _____ _____ over and play dead.
        11   10   8   8

❸ If you pick me up, I will _____ _____ _____ _____ limp.
                             6   1   9   5

❹ If you put me back down, I will flip over on my
   _____ _____ _____ _____.
    2   1   3   7

❺ I am a _____ _____ _____ _____ _____ _____ _____
   snake. 6   10   5   9   10   12   4

Subtraction 0–20

Time to Hatch

Write a subtraction problem for each picture showing how may eggs are left to hatch.

| 1 | 15 – _____ = _____ |

| 2 | 18 – _____ = _____ |

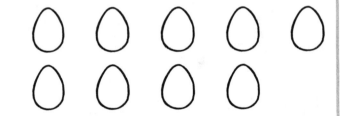

| 3 | 14 – _____ = _____ |

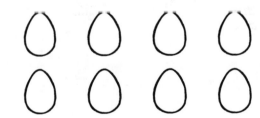

| 4 | 9 – _____ = _____ |

Up and Away

Solve each subtraction problem. Use the Color Code to color the picture.

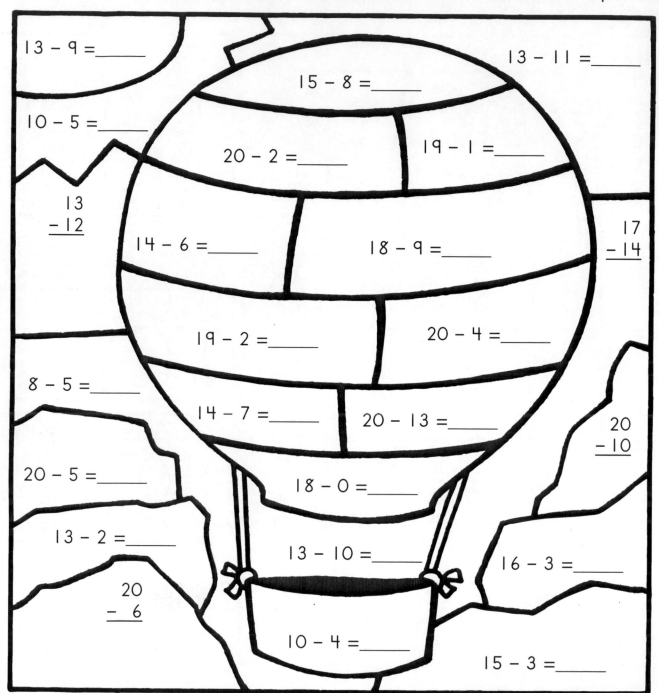

13 − 9 = _____

15 − 8 = _____

13 − 11 = _____

10 − 5 = _____

20 − 2 = _____

19 − 1 = _____

13
−12
_____

14 − 6 = _____

18 − 9 = _____

17
−14
_____

19 − 2 = _____

20 − 4 = _____

8 − 5 = _____

14 − 7 = _____

20 − 13 = _____

20
−10
_____

20 − 5 = _____

18 − 0 = _____

13 − 2 = _____

13 − 10 = _____

16 − 3 = _____

20
− 6
_____

10 − 4 = _____

15 − 3 = _____

Color Code	blue — 1, 2, 3	red — 7, 8, 9	brown — 13, 14, 15
	yellow — 4, 5, 6	green — 10, 11, 12	purple — 16, 17, 18

How Many Cookies Are Left?

Read each word problem. Cross out the cookies that have been eaten.
Write a subtraction sentence to show how many cookies are left.

1

Jessica baked 20 cookies.
Her brother ate 8 cookies.
How many cookies are left?

_____ – _____ = _____

2

Dad made 20 cookies.
The twins ate 6 cookies.
How many cookies are left?

_____ – _____ = _____

3

Grandma made 20 cookies.
Her friends ate 12 cookies.
How many cookies are left?

_____ – _____ = _____

Garden Facts

Solve the subtraction problems in each row of vegetables.

1

29 – 9 = _____   27 – 4 = _____   30 – 20 = _____

2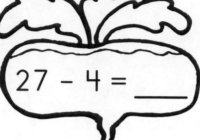

17
– 6
___

29
– 5
___

30
– 2
___

3

28 – 6 = _____   10 – 10 = _____   18 – 3 = _____

4

29
– 3
___

26
– 4
___

12
– 4
___

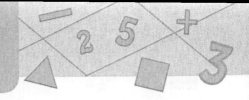

Turtle Practice

Start with the number in the center of the shell. Subtract the number in the middle ring. Write the answer in the outer ring.

Subtract the Shapes

Count the shapes in each set and draw the answer in the box on the right. Write the subtraction problem below the shapes in each row.

1

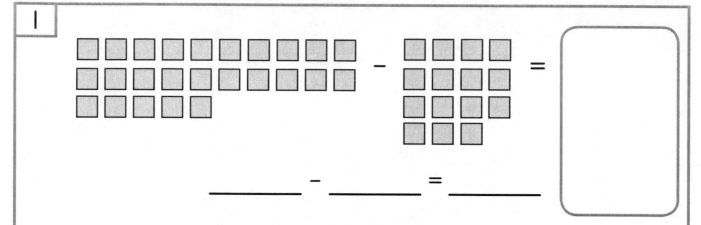

_____ - _____ = _____

2

_____ - _____ = _____

3

_____ - _____ = _____

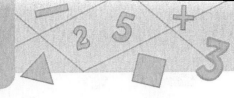

Addition and Subtraction Review 0–10

Solve the problems. Pay careful attention to the addition and subtraction signs.

1 $3 + 1 =$ _____

2 $0 + 2 =$ _____

3 $4 - 2 =$ _____

4 $3 - 3 =$ _____

5 $1 + 2 =$ _____

6 $3 + 0 =$ _____

7 $5 - 4 =$ _____

8 $2 - 0 =$ _____

9 $5 - 3 =$ _____

10
$$\begin{array}{r} 7 \\ +3 \\ \hline \end{array}$$

11
$$\begin{array}{r} 4 \\ +3 \\ \hline \end{array}$$

12
$$\begin{array}{r} 8 \\ -3 \\ \hline \end{array}$$

13
$$\begin{array}{r} 10 \\ -6 \\ \hline \end{array}$$

14
$$\begin{array}{r} 4 \\ +6 \\ \hline \end{array}$$

15
$$\begin{array}{r} 6 \\ +0 \\ \hline \end{array}$$

16
$$\begin{array}{r} 9 \\ -4 \\ \hline \end{array}$$

17
$$\begin{array}{r} 7 \\ +2 \\ \hline \end{array}$$

18
$$\begin{array}{r} 10 \\ -8 \\ \hline \end{array}$$

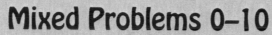

Addition and Subtraction Review 0–10

Check the addition and subtraction signs and solve the problems.

1   4 + 1 = _____

2   3 + 0 = _____

3   5 – 5 = _____

4   4 + 3 = _____

5   6 – 2 = _____

6   5 + 5 = _____

7
$$\begin{array}{r} 2 \\ +\,8 \\ \hline \end{array}$$

8
$$\begin{array}{r} 8 \\ -\,5 \\ \hline \end{array}$$

9
$$\begin{array}{r} 10 \\ +\,0 \\ \hline \end{array}$$

10
$$\begin{array}{r} 10 \\ -\,7 \\ \hline \end{array}$$

11
$$\begin{array}{r} 6 \\ +\,3 \\ \hline \end{array}$$

12
$$\begin{array}{r} 9 \\ -\,8 \\ \hline \end{array}$$

13
$$\begin{array}{r} 7 \\ -\,5 \\ \hline \end{array}$$

14
$$\begin{array}{r} 6 \\ +\,2 \\ \hline \end{array}$$

15
$$\begin{array}{r} 4 \\ +\,4 \\ \hline \end{array}$$

16
$$\begin{array}{r} 9 \\ -\,7 \\ \hline \end{array}$$

17
$$\begin{array}{r} 8 \\ -\,8 \\ \hline \end{array}$$

18
$$\begin{array}{r} 5 \\ +\,3 \\ \hline \end{array}$$

Addition and Subtraction Review 0–20

Check the addition and subtraction signs and solve the problems.

1
```
  10
-  5
```

2
```
   8
- 7
```

3
```
 13
+ 0
```

4
```
   7
+ 6
```

5
```
  11
-  7
```

6
```
 16
- 5
```

7
```
   3
+ 9
```

8
```
 12
+ 4
```

9   3 + 8 = _____

10   3 + 9 = _____

11   16 – 4 = _____

12   12 – 8 = _____

13   16 + 3 = _____

14   13 + 4 = _____

15
```
 12
-  5
```

16
```
 18
- 6
```

17
```
 20
-  7
```

18   15 + 5 = _____

19   12 – 10 = _____

20   19 – 8 = _____

Addition and Subtraction Review 0–20

Check the addition and subtraction signs and solve the problems.

1
```
   2
   4
 + 6
────
```

2
```
   3
   3
 + 3
────
```

3
```
   5
   4
 + 1
────
```

4
```
   8
   3
 + 6
────
```

5   15 – 7 = ____

6   20 – 7 = ____

7   14 – 7 = ____

8   12 – 7 = ____

9   10 + 7 = ____

10   13 – 6 = ____

11
```
   6
   3
   4
 + 3
────
```

12
```
   7
   6
   4
 + 3
────
```

13
```
   9
   3
   2
 + 2
────
```

14
```
  12
   3
   4
 + 1
────
```

Addition and Subtraction Review 0–30

Check the addition and subtraction signs and solve the problems.

1

13 – 9 = ____

2

20 – 3 = ____

3

13 – 6 = ____

4

```
  14
+  4
```

5

```
  11
+  5
```

6

```
  10
+  8
```

7

15 + 3 = ____

8

20 – 13 = ____

9

8 + 5 = ____

10

```
  9
+7
```

11

```
  20
– 13
```

12

```
  8
+5
```

13

```
25
+3
```

14

```
  26
– 13
```

15

```
  14
+ 15
```

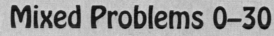

Mixed Problems 0–30

Addition and Subtraction Review 0–30

Check the addition and subtraction signs and solve the problems.

1 16 – 10 = _____

2 19 – 7 = _____

3 15 – 6 = _____

4
```
   18
 +10
```

5
```
   21
 +  5
```

6
```
   20
 +  9
```

7 18 + 6 = _____

8 30 – 15 = _____

9 18 + 8 = _____

10
```
   19
  +7
```

11
```
   23
 –13
```

12
```
   18
  +5
```

13
```
   26
  +3
```

14
```
   27
 –13
```

15
```
   15
 +13
```

Answer Key

Page 13

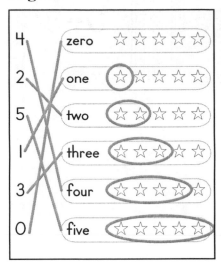

Page 14

four   three
two   zero
one   five

Page 15

Check that numbers match the number of birds.

Page 16

Check that items match the numbers.

Page 17

Check that colors match the dot codes.

Page 18

Check that each dog has one of each type of item.

Page 19

Check that each closet has an equal number of items.

Page 20

Check student lines.

Page 21

3 guitars
4 drums
Check coloring of each instrument.

Page 22

sailboats	3
sea stars	4
pails	3
seagulls	5
balls	5
umbrellas	2

Page 23

3 sets
Check coloring of each set of fish.

Page 24

X on bird; 4
X on maraca; 5
X on banana; 5

Page 25

1. 4
2. 3
3. 5
4. 2

Page 26

1. 2
2. 5
3. 3
4. 4
5. 2
6. 4

Page 27

1. 1
2. 4
3. 3
4. 4
5. 5 (circled)

Page 28

1 triangle
2 squares
3 circles
4 rectangles
5 rhombuses (diamonds)
no ovals

Page 29

5 circles
4 rectangles
3 triangles
5 rhombuses
4 squares
2 ovals

Page 30

Check numbers in drawings.

Page 31

Check lines for matches.

Page 32

Check page for accuracy.

Page 33

6 buttons circled
4 buttons circled
5 buttons circled

Page 34

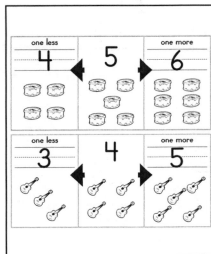

Page 35

fish	5
whales	1
eels	3
sharks	2
clams	4
dolphins	2
octopus	1
sea stars	5

Page 36

1 cow
5 chickens
3 sheep
2 horses

Page 44

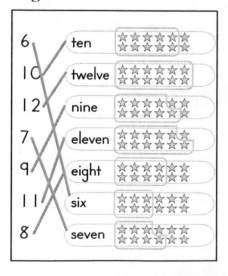

Page 45

Page 46

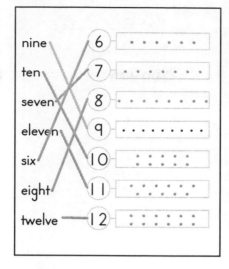

Page 47

Check coloring for accuracy.

Page 48

8 balls
9 buckets
12 crayons

Page 49

9 diamond (rhombus) buttons
12 oval buttons
7 rectangle buttons

Page 50

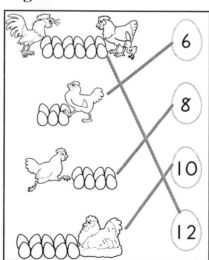

Page 51

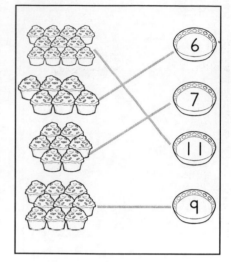

Page 52

1. 7
2. 6
3. 11
4. 8

Page 53

12 shells
8 flip flops
9 sea stars

Page 54

Check that the correct number of shapes have been drawn.

Page 55

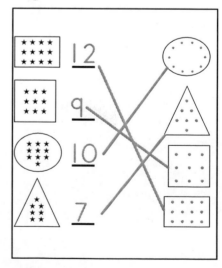

Dot patterns will vary.

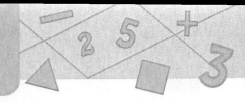

Page 56

4 horns
3 drums
2 guitars
9 instruments

Page 57

3 space men
9 rockets
7 aliens
12 stars

Page 58

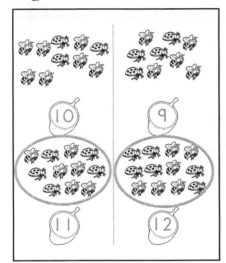

Page 59

9 candles - circle cake
6 candles - circle cake
11 candles - circle cake

Page 60

Page 61

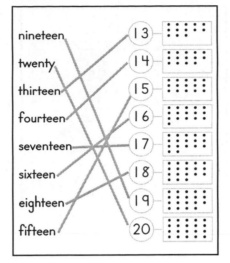

Page 62

1. 13
2. 17
3. 19
4. 15

Page 63

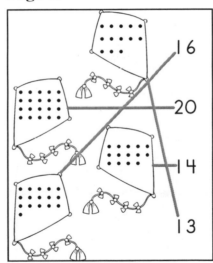

Page 64

Check coloring for accuracy.

Page 65

Check colors.

Page 66

13 14 15	7 8 9	15 16 17
24 25 26	18 19 20	17 18 19
12 13 14	10 11 12	16 17 18
4 5 6	25 26 27	11 12 13
2 3 4	9 10 11	27 28 29
22 23 24	14 15 16	28 29 30

Check that odd and even
numbers were circled correctly.

Page 67

30
22
29
25
Check page for accuracy circling
stars.

Page 68

1. 21
2. 30
3. 27
4. 23

Page 69

1. 2 tens and 2 ones = 22
2. 1 tens and 5 ones = 15
3. 2 tens and 6 ones = 26
4. 2 tens and 8 ones = 28

Page 70

1. 2 tens and 3 ones = 23
2. 2 tens and 9 ones = 29
3. 1 tens and 6 ones = 16
4. 2 tens and 8 ones = 28

Page 71

1. 2 + 1 = 3
2. 2 + 2 = 4
3. 3 + 1 = 4
4. 2 + 3 = 5

Page 72

1. 3 + 2 = 5
2. 1 + 3 = 4
3. 4 + 1 = 5

Page 73

5
5
4
3
Check page for accuracy drawing shapes.

Page 74

In the basket: 3+2, 1+4, 0+5

Page 75

1. 2 + 2 = 4
2. 3 + 2 = 5
3. 2 + 1 = 3

Page 76

1. 3 + 3 = 6
2. 4 + 3 = 7
3. 4 + 4 = 8
4. 5 + 1 = 6

Page 77

1. 3 + 5 = 8
2. 4 + 2 = 6

Page 78

Check coloring for accuracy.

Page 79

1. 9
2. 7
3. 8
4. 4
5. 10
6. 6

Page 80

1. 6 + 3 = 9
2. 4 + 3 = 7
3. 5 + 5 = 10

Page 81

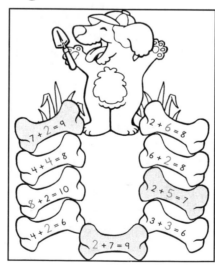

Page 82

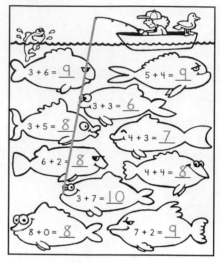

Page 83

5
8
2
0
1
6
3
7
4
Mystery number: 9

Page 84

1. 9
2. 10
3. 6
4. 9
5. Answers will vary.
Check student shapes for accuracy.

Page 85

1. 4 + 4 = 8
2. 3 + 2 = 5
3. 3 + 6 = 9
4. 7 + 3 = 10
5. 8 + 4 = 12

Page 86

1. $5 + 5 = 10$
2. $2 + 1 = 3$
3. $2 + 4 = 6$
4. $6 + 6 = 12$
5. $2 + 3 = 5$
6. $4 + 5 = 9$
7. 1
8. 6
9. 4

Page 87

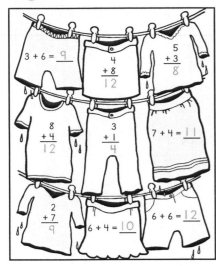
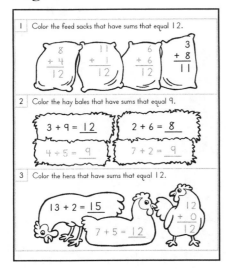

Page 88

Page 89

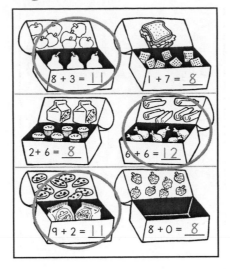

Page 90

1. 9
2. $3 + 6 = 9$
3. $3 + 9 = 12$
4. $4 + 3 = 7$
5. $5 + 6 = 11$
6. $7 + 8 = 15$
7. $4 + 9 = 13$

Page 91

1. 4
2. 4
3. 9

Check student drawings.

Page 92

Page 93

row 1	9	13	8
row 2	11	15	10
row 3	7	14	12

Lucky Backpack 10 (circled)

Page 94

Page 95

Page 96

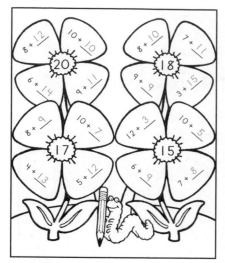

Page 97

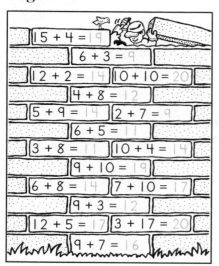

Page 98

1. 9
2. 3
3. 4
4. 12
5. 10
6. 5
7. 8
8. 7
9. 6
10. 2
11. 0
12. 1

Secret Message

four plus seven equals eleven

$4 + 7 = 11$

Page 99

1. yes; $10 + 10 = 20$
2. $4 + 4 + 4 = 12$

Check student drawings.

Page 100

Check coloring.

Page 101

Page 102

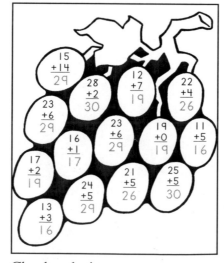

Check coloring.

Page 103

1. $9 + 10 = 19$
2. $10 + 10 + 6 = 26$
3. $9 + 20 = 29$
4. $11 + 9 + 2 = 22$

Page 104

1. 3
2. 2
3. 1
4. 5
5. 4

Page 105

1. $5 - 1 = 4$
2. $3 - 2 = 1$
3. $4 - 1 = 3$
4. $4 - 2 = 2$

Page 106

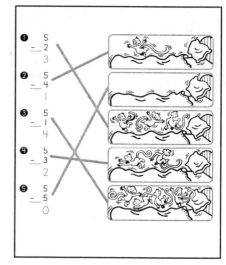

Page 107

1. $4 - 1 = 3$
2. $4 - 2 = 2$
3. $5 - 3 = 2$
4. $5 - 4 = 1$
5. $5 - 2 = 3$
6. $4 - 3 = 1$
7. $5 - 1 = 4$
8. $3 - 2 = 1$

Page 108

1. 2, 1, 3; bat
2. 0, 1, 3; cat
3. 0, 1, 2; cab

Page 109

1. 4, 2; 6 − 4 = 2
2. 2, 4; 6 − 2 = 4
3. 3, 3; 6 − 3 = 3
4. 5, 1; 6 − 5 = 1
5. 6, 0; 6 − 6 = 0

Page 110

1. 4
2. 2
3. 5
4. 5
5. 4
6. 4

Page 111

1. 9 − 6 = 3
2. 9 − 4 = 5
3. 9 − 5 = 4
4. 9 − 8 = 1
5. 9 − 3 = 6
6. 9 − 7 = 2

Page 112

❶ How many more ants are there than worms?
  9 − 6 = 3
❷ How many more ants are there than spiders?
  9 − 5 = 4
❸ How many more worms are there than spiders?
  6 − 5 = 1

Page 113

1. 9 − 3 = 6
2. 6 − 3 = 3
3. 8 − 4 = 4

Page 114

1. 7   4. 4
2. 4   5. 3
3. 3   6. 1

Check student lines.

Page 115

Check the colors on rainbow.

Page 116

1. 10 − 2 = 8 or 10 − 8 = 2
   8
2. 8 − 3 = 5 or 8 − 5 = 3
   5
3. 9 − 5 = 4 or 9 − 4 = 5
   4

Page 117

1. 6; 12 − 6 = 6
2. 4; 12 − 4 = 8
3. 8; 12 − 8 = 4

Page 118

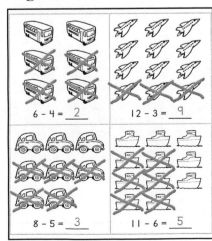

6 − 4 = 2   12 − 3 = 9

8 − 5 = 3   11 − 6 = 5

Page 119

1. 6
2. 4
3. 5
4. 2

Check items crossed out.

Page 120

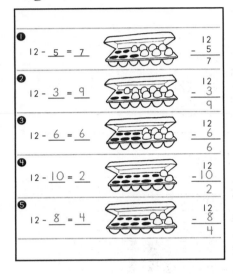

❶ 12 − 5 = 7   12 − 5 = 7
❷ 12 − 3 = 9   12 − 3 = 9
❸ 12 − 6 = 6   12 − 6 = 6
❹ 12 − 10 = 2   12 − 10 = 2
❺ 12 − 8 = 4   12 − 8 = 4

Page 121

5, 1, 2, 4, 4, 2, 3, 6
swimming

Page 122

Check the coloring on the turtle.

Page 123

1. 14 – 3 = 11
2. 13 – 5 = 8
3. 15 – 6 = 9
4. 12 – 2 = 10

Page 124

5	11
1	7
12	3
2	8
9	6
4	10

1. nose
2. roll
3. hang
4. back
5. hognose

Page 125

1. 15 – 5 = 10
2. 18 – 9 = 9
3. 14 – 6 = 8
4. 9 – 3 = 6

Page 126

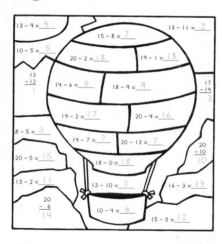

Check that colors match the number codes.

Page 127

1. 20 – 8 = 12
2. 20 – 6 = 14
3. 20 – 12 = 8

Page 128

1. 20, 23, 10
2. 11, 24, 28
3. 22, 0, 15
4. 26, 22, 8

Page 129

Page 130

1. 25 – 15 = 10
2. 20 – 12 = 8
3. 30 – 15 = 15

Page 131

1. 4	10. 10
2. 2	11. 7
3. 2	12. 5
4. 0	13. 4
5. 3	14. 10
6. 3	15. 6
7. 1	16. 5
8. 2	17. 9
9. 2	18. 2

Page 132

1. 5	10. 3
2. 3	11. 9
3. 0	12. 1
4. 7	13. 2
5. 4	14. 8
6. 10	15. 8
7. 10	16. 2
8. 3	17. 0
9. 10	18. 8

Page 133

1. 5	11. 12
2. 1	12. 4
3. 13	13. 19
4. 13	14. 17
5. 4	15. 7
6. 11	16. 12
7. 12	17. 13
8. 16	18. 20
9. 11	19. 2
10. 12	20. 11

Page 134

1. 12	8. 5
2. 9	9. 17
3. 10	10. 7
4. 17	11. 16
5. 8	12. 20
6. 13	13. 16
7. 7	14. 20

Page 135

1 4	9. 13
2. 17	10. 16
3. 7	11. 7
4. 18	12. 13
5. 16	13. 28
6. 18	14. 13
7. 18	15. 29
8. 7	

Page 136

1. 6
2. 12
3. 9
4. 28
5. 26
6. 29
7. 24
8. 15
9. 26
10. 26
11. 10
12. 23
13. 29
14. 14
15. 28